a seed within

a seed within

Bruce Kauffman

Hidden Brook Press

First Edition

Hidden Brook Press
www.HiddenBrookPress.com
writers@HiddenBrookPress.com

Copyright © 2013 Hidden Brook Press
Copyright © 2013 Bruce Kauffman

All rights revert to the author. All rights for book, layout and design remain with Hidden Brook Press. No part of this book may be reproduced except by a reviewer who may quote brief passages in a review. The use of any part of this publication reproduced, transmitted in any form or by any means, electronic, mechanical, photocopied, recorded or otherwise stored in a retrieval system without prior written consent of the publisher is an infringement of the copyright law.

a seed within
by Bruce Kauffman

Cover Photograph – Eleanor Leonne Bennett
Layout and Design – Richard M. Grove
Cover Design – Richard M. Grove

Typeset in Calibri
Printed and bound in USA

Library and Archives Canada Cataloguing in Publication

Kauffman, Bruce, author
    A seed within / Bruce Kauffman.

Poems.
ISBN 978-1-897475-99-7 (pbk.)

    I. Title.

PS8621.A685S44 2013   C811'.6   C2013-901684-8

From far a light, maybe a hill ranch
remote and unvisited, beams on the horizon
when we pass; then it is gone.
For the rest of our lives that far place
waits; it's an increment, one more
hollow that slips by out there, almost
a gift, an acquaintance taken away.

Still, beyond all ranches the deep
night waits, breathing when we breathe,
always ready to offer new light,
over and over, so long as we search
for something so faint most people
won't know, even when it is found.

William Stafford, "Deep Light"
from "Who Are You Really, Wanderer?"
Honeybrook Press, 1993

Preface

This shorter collection of poetry is an expansion of my previously published chapbook, *seed* (The Plowman Press, 2005).

There is a presumption on my part that the original press closed its doors shortly after my chapbook was published and I was not able to either connect or contact that publisher when I attempted to obtain additional copies of the chapbook. I would, however, like to acknowledge that press and say that it was wonderful working with them as my first chapbook of poetry came out, and to give them publishing credit for what is a substantial part of this work.

Hidden Brook Press approached me with an interest to publish an expanded version of the chapbook, so that it could be contained in a perfect-bound book. I expressed a desire to allow those poems to reappear.

This book is divided into three sections: the "prologue", "seed", and the "epilogue". The first and last section, somewhat themed, act as both an expansion of and cover for the middle section that was the chapbook itself, and laid out exactly as it was in 2005.

My thanks to Tai Grove, publisher of Hidden Brook Press, for his invitation to allow this to again come to light in a broader way.

Contents

***prologue*:**
   years – *p. 1*
   whisper – *p. 2*
   cracks – *p. 3*
   day – *p. 5*
   answered – *p. 6*

***seed*:**
   cage – *p. 9*
   stone – *p. 11*
   late afternoon – *p. 13*
   lake – *p. 15*
   thirst – *p. 17*
   isolation – *p. 19*
   in the morning – *p. 20*
   eulogy – *p. 21*
   alive – *p. 23*
   fear – *p. 24*
   first – *p. 25*
   in another day – *p. 26*
   shadowless – *p. 28*
   torrent – *p. 30*
   gifts – *p. 32*
   rain – *p. 33*

wind – *p. 35*
silence – *p. 36*
colour – *p. 37*
coincidence – *p. 38*
friendship – *p. 39*
rolling stone – *p. 40*
dream – *p. 42*

***epilogue*:**
freedom – *p. 45*
october – *p. 47*
thread – *p. 50*
fragments – *p. 52*
end – *p. 57*
tether – *p. 61*

Author Bio – *p. 62*
Front Cover Photographer Bio – *p. 65*

prologue

years

sitting
in this same spot
exactly one year
      later

knowing even
that time
changes
      nothing

but i can
tell you
sitting here
now

how all the words
in every language,
then but smoke and haze
hanging low
      to the ground,
have now
given way
      to the warmth

of the endless breath
      behind

whisper

the days fall
        more softly
        now
under
        the shadow
        of these clouds
i, wrapped
        within the shade
        of your memory
        of sun

here
in this new light
the shadows
        of gull
        of the crow
        the eagle fly

        without body
        and

fly above
in your whispers
        painted
        across the sky

cracks

i watch
as the tip of
my finger
runs slowly
      along
      on top
of table's edge
tracing the crack
between surface

these lines
      between

an index finger

gently obscuring
      division
      boundary
slowly blurring
      definition
      separation

a finger

cosmically
compassionately
      leaving itself
      behind

a smooth surface
concealing
bonding
that line
      where crack
      once was and

in its place
a now polished surface
of new fresh skin

day

i hear the sun
calling
      behind the clouds

its warm breath
      searching
for believing
      remembering ears

opaque clouds
      forgetting on
      one side the sun

      finally parting
      to the memory
           of day

answered

coming to this place

the same place
i always come
early
at dawn
on sunday mornings

passively open
expecting
    nothing

until the rising sun
pulls my attention
from the street that was
as i look up into a pale blue sky and

from its centre
the calling
of an almost invisible
    crescent moon and
in its wave of languages
raining down and washing
through
come the whispers
of all other eyes
tied watching

and come the answers
    to all questions lost

seed

cage

you cage
this bird
    foreign to here

and you clip
    its wing
believing
    she would not
    remember
        tree
believing
    she would
    forget
        the tree
        from where
            she came
    forget
        the seed
        insects
            she used to eat

and you believe
that in the morning
    as she sings

        she sings
                for you

but she sings
        with eyes
        closed

        singing back
        to dew laden
                branches of
                mornings
                        before wire
                        before wall

stone

how long
      do the pictures
      hang
until they
      run out of
            words

until they
      bleed
            into the paint
            on the wall

until everything
      else in the room
            rises and falls
            moves and waits
                  around them
                  without them

until all of
      picture's pieces
            of flesh
            of moisture
                  fade and
                  fall away

    until only
        stone eyes
        are left
            watching dust
            covered absence
                hanging on
            whispers of the echoed
            water on the other
                side slipping
                off leaves
                      in a forgotten
                      forest
                            on a desert
                            morning

late afternoon

hiding here
    in the shade
    of the tall grass
        remembering all
        the setting suns
            and one full
            moon rising

the light
of this day
    too now
beginning
    to thin

the shadows
    falling
the earth
    accepting
    them all

the shadows
    of vultures
    and doves
        believing
        they each
            the same

as they
both fall
	on me now

one as a gift
	already is
the other
	a gift
	waiting
		to be

lake

I will tell you
the colour
    of the lake
    in morning
        of how it changes
        with the sky
            the season
        of how the ice
        comes first
            to the shore
            as if unsure

and I will tell you
how
    to reach it in
    trails of different
    shadows and shades
        off the branches
        of the trees
            in the morning
            and the afternoon and
    trails at night
        cast by the stars
        and pieces of
            the moon

and I will tell you
well enough
    how to reach it
    without wasting
        words

and know that
as I tell you
    you will find it
        and you will see
    and I will not
        be there

thirst

We drink from the basin
      the river basin
      the river bed,
that same basin which
spawned a civilization
      and drowned a child.
Perhaps what we mistake
for river is but a pocket
      full of tears.

There is a forest
with but a corner burnt
and from a distance
      barren.
Yet distance conceals
a greener grass, a field
of berries more wild and sweet
      with the wisdom and
      taste for sun.

We praise the morning,
search for light and
      watch the shadows fall,
forgetting that fear was
neither borne nor vanquished
      in darkness -
night's veil concealing
only obstacles
cannot contain
      the passion.

How far, how long can we
look into the eyes of eternity,
      infinity
before we close our own and
look away?
And in an instant realize
she lies back as far
      the other way.

And, now, which way
to turn?

isolation

comes
    the last
    of the green
        days

comes
    the river
    washing

comes
    the grey
    sky in the
        short days
    the black
    nights
        forgetting moon

comes
    the wind
        without word
        without music

        comes the doors
        swinging forward
            back forward
            back with

                no one
                watching

in the morning

this morning
I took an
empty clear glass
  to the lake

I, still unaware
  of the beginning
  of things
still lost in the illusion
  of boundaries
  of lines

I, calling out
  to the green
  in these grey
    times

I, waiting
  for the lake
  to fill
    my glass

I, sitting here
beside the water
  with an open
    glass
I, sitting here

  in the rain

eulogy

an old crow
  sits above
  a light post
    over a street

her body scarred
  eyes clouded
    sight having flown
    in a different direction
      in an earlier part
      of the day

feathers wilting
  into a duller colour
down ruffled
  to hide her open
  pieces of skin
    exposed

as she closes her eyes
  to the heat
  of the day

raises her head
        to the sky and
        with beak slowly
                opening calls
                out from the depth
                        of her chest within

remembering
        another lifetime
        without wings

                and missing it

alive

comes the skin
      of a new day
believing in
      itself
believing in
      touch
believing in
      its own colour
      at dawn
           enough

to give its
own colour up
      to the sun
      to the cloud
      the night
           coming

to give it up
      to all other
           skin

and it patiently
watching, waiting
      for every thing

asking for
      nothing

fear

I fear nothing
      except, perhaps,

    forgetting

        emptiness

first

before the music
      there was but
      discordant noise

before the rhythm
      there were but
      errant notes

before the wings
      was the feather-less
      hatchling

before the sky
      was branch
            mud and straw
      and

as I look
this morning
in each direction
      at every thing
this thought-

      before true sight
      there is this

in another day

waiting
        for the quiet
        to remember
                who it was
                come back
                      to itself

ghosts
        not yet here
        already passing
                not yet knowing
                what they are

the ink
the blood
        disappears

                the water
                the dust
                      remain
                as

birds overhead
walking on air
    with their wings
aware
realizing
    that we call that
    a different name
        and

when we
have forgotten
    all the words
    in all the languages

        the new birds
        will still fly
            remembering
            even this

shadowless

a shadow
        hides a face
        that is not
                looking back

in another country
sheets of
        glass and ice
        slide one soul
                into another

                and away
                from someone
                      else

in another time
when we
have forgotten
        the words
                we will hear
                their echoes
                      and not remember

today
        waited patiently
        nearly forever
                for our coming

                and wrapped
                within its own
                        echo
                passes
                        as we are
                              looking away

torrent

comes
      the rain
as if it
      knew
            knows
a world
      and a heart
            wait to be
            cleansed

waterfalls
rivers
      knew of
      its coming
            before the
            shadows of
            clouds
                  carpeted themselves
                  on bank
                        and rock

but how long
       does it take
       a teardrop
              to roll
              across a
              continent

and how long
       before
       it reaches
              there
              did she
              taste
                      its salt

gifts

those, these gifts
     of life
          we take
          for granted -

               scent
               light
               sound
               touch
                    breath

rain

you, carrying
the love
    of children
watching sides
    disappear but
    edges sharpening
        grow

you, feeling years
    of years

fearing the coming
    too soon or
    too late or
    too long with
        worlds sliding
        walls falling
           behind you

you, watching and
now questioning
    all things as you
    feel the earth roll
        beneath you

you, who ran
through the streets
      the pastures
      as a child
you
now just learning
      how to crawl
      on this new water
           of time

wind

the wind
    believes
the shadow
    holds on
        to it
    does not
        let it go
        to the light

it believes
    it is still
    yesterday
        coming back
        to itself
            and still

cannot explain
this darkness
    approaching
        without moon

in this still
calm
        of stars falling
        and the black sky
            moving
            both farther
                away
            and within

silence

as you sit
alone
        in the darkness
        in the low part
                of a snow covered
                night

and you can
truly sense
        the peace
        the stillness
        the fullness
        the softness
                of silence

you understand
at last that
        the opposite
        of silence is
                neither sound
                nor noise

but instead
        emptiness

colour

before
>the places
>had names

>and the paths
>were circles
>>wearing wheels

>and the sun
>spoke
>>in tongues of white light
>>in the language of absence
>>>sending the colours
>>>out, and
>>>calling the shadows
>>>back

and in that time
>colour not merely
>painted on surface
>>but translucent
>and known to itself
>and every other thing
 not by name
>>but by texture, instead

coincidence

this
those
these
      points in time
           and space
where two
      lines cross

with you
I
we
      standing there

      believing there
      is no reason
           no explanation
           why

and it is
only because
      we fail to see

we forget to call
      it destiny

and call it
      instead
           coincidence

friendship

friendship
      is the water
      in our lives
coming with
      moving against
      the dryness
            of calendar
                    clock

comes first
      as the dew

then
      the rain
           the river
                 and

the old water
always rolling
      first
the new water
always coming
      last and

            purifying
            that which
                  already is

rolling stone

a stone
       tumbling
       rolling

for the
       life of
       rock

for the
       embrace of
       gravity

for that
       piece of
       earth
              holding
              shaping
                     the crevice
                     of the other
                     half of
                            its heart

```
until it
rests
            nestles
            in that other
                    wearing the
                    shape of itself
                            and

finally

finally
        welcomes
        the moss
```

dream

you call me
    now
on the backside
    of the other
    words that
        were
in the echoes
    of another
    language

the moon
wears them
    all

and you tell
me about
    old dreams
        weeping
    new dreams
        whispering

and I now
    with the moon
the only one left
    believing still
    in them all

epilogue

freedom

you speak
of freedom
      now

you having left

a blue sky
and that vastness
you once felt
not just above
      but encircling
      earth
      you
      itself

you having left

every colour
in every field
      with colours
      yet waiting

every tree touched

every feather
      believed in and

you then
caught all of this
in your net
and carefully
placed it in a clear jar
carried it back
through the door
into the walls
      you have always
      known and

some nights
now
in its quietest part
      you believe
      you still hear

the sky
the feathers
the fields
the colours
the words
      falling gently outside
      with the rain

october

marked once
my entry
into this world
        this time

birth
again
        now
in autumn
as the soft music
of the breeze
paints itself across
each leaf
        burgundy, red
        yellow, gold

noon sky
pastel sun

shadows fuller, deeper
than themselves

air wearing
dusk's texture
        golden colour

breeze wrapping
around days'
    intermittent grey
and evenings'
    harvest moon

moon
peering back down
beneath, behind
between
    black leafless limbs

and it was here
this place
this time
i was borne
    in another
    country
there, when
the grains of sand
in an ever-rocking hourglass
    were each engraved
    with a life waiting

waiting

waiting in that cosmic
        hourglass and
they all
each
waiting for
the gravity
of a soul
        to let it fall through

thread

with air and water watching

each of us
endlessly moving
along this path
      from that which was
      to that which is

remembering
      only pieces
      of earth and sky

pulling behind each
a single blue thread frayed
      from the ball of all thread
      of lifetimes woven

and each of us
the needle guiding
this thread
this colour
        into this tapestry
        of days and nights and
leaving again
at the end
        a single blue thread

        hanging, waiting
        to be tied to that

        next lifetime coming

fragments

i.

deep inside
       within the soul
       within the heart
       behind the mind

images

       reflections of

this universe
       of leaves and
shadows cast
       on opposing walls

the wind
wrapping itself
       around tree
drifting the
       fallen snow
scurrying the
       dusty road

needing to prove
    itself

    to show

    to show

        to show

ii.

i wait

i stand
within
this cosmic breath
exhaled

enveloping
swirling
tangled memory
    with hope

in the perfumed scent
of childlike faith of
all that appears as not
is
will be

crystalline breath
inhaled

exhaled back
into
    voiceless time
    waiting

iii.

each of us
calendars of water-colour
paint on glass
      in the pouring rain

yellow lines
on amber background
      behind a golden veil

charcoal stillness
behind silhouettes of
      trees at dusk

breath's fogged vapour
within gentle snow falling
      in the stillness at dawn

each of us
innocuous

as a whisper
carried in the breeze
blowing
slowly

across the earth
> for others to hear
> with an uncovered ear

and still blowing slowly
across the earth
> our whisper returns

> within a silent echo
> to remember
> to remind and

a memory fuller
> in our then introspection

and fuller again
> in the choral reflection
> of all whisper shared

end

these walls
      stained
in the pastel paint
of ancestral
      memory

you
sitting within

you, alone
      the last
      of your seed
can hear
the grey sky   calling

outside these
silent echoes
of thought
off paint
      and stain

you,
your weathered hands
holding the end
of this string
of carefully threaded seed

a simple piece of string
passed from first
        generation down
threaded seeds
one for each
        all your ancestors' lives

and now you
with humble
        almost feeble
fingers clumsily
        adding now your own
        to the worn string
                and

you hearing
ancestral voice
all but
each
        separate
        distinct
rising up
out of each seed

and you
surrounded by
these half muffled
sounds
  of all their voices
  all their visions
    all the stories
until
the paint
the stains
the air
the voices
  fold into
  each other

and within
as you sit
you sense ever
so
loosely
gradually
effortlessly
passively
all of your weight
as you begin
  to slide
  to sink
  to fall back
slumped into chair and

then
in an instant
      of clarity
in an instant
      of silence

the paint
the stains
the air
      all take on
      one the same
           lucid colour

and the grey sky
opens

you becoming
weightless
as you slowly
outside consciousness
      close your eyes

and with a body's
no longer directed
fingers
      the string
      sags
           teetering

      then falls from your
      lifeless hand

tether

it is through
this looking glass
that i travel
this hole
      within whole

where
the stars
the wind
the sun
      have already been

they
already each
a hundred thousand
years ahead
as they pave
      the way
as they rest
      outside of time
as they have
already spread
      the tails of their
      coats backward

for us

to grasp
at tethered threads

      and follow

Bruce Kauffman lives in Kingston, Ontario and is a poet, writer, editor and workshop facilitator. A chapbook of his poetry, *seed* (The Plowman), was published in 2005, a stand-alone poem, "streets" (Thee Hellbox Press) was published in 2009 and his first full collection of poetry,
The Texture of Days, in Ash and Leaf (Hidden Brook Press), launched in January 2013. His latest two books, *a seed within* (an expansion of his original chapbook) and *The Silence Before the Whisper Come*s, both with Hidden Brook Press, will also launch in 2013.

His work has appeared in numerous periodicals and anthologies, including a book review in *The Antigonish Review* (fall /2010) for John Pigeau's *The Nothing Waltz* (Hidden Brook Press). His poetry has also appeared in two plays, *The Garbage and the Flowers* (2008) and *A Moveable Feast* (2009). His poem "destiny", appearing in his first collection, was shortlisted in the 1995 Poiesis Poetry Competition.

In 1997/1998 he was research editor and volunteer coordinator for a poetry short collection and reference manual, the Poiesis Poetry Guide (1998). In 2011 he coordinated and edited That Not Forgotten (Hidden Brook Press), a 400 page poetry/short fiction anthology of 118 locally tied poets and authors, launched in September 2012.

In May 2010, he began hosting a weekly spoken word radio show on CFRC 101.9fm (Queen's University, Kingston, ON) called "finding a voice" and now also hosts a blogspace for that show at: http://findingavoiceoncfrcfm.wordpress.com/. As well, he hosts a monthly open mic reading series called "poetry @ the artel" (launched in May, 2009), and now facilitates a quarterly series of "stream of consciousness" writing workshops in Kingston with plans to expand to outlying areas.

He is a member of a local writers group. He joined the Wintergreen Studios Press Advisory Board as Acquisitions and Poetry Editor in July, 2012 and in August, 2012 became the Canadian Editor of CCLA's *The Ambassador*. He is currently editing other work and working on his next poetry manuscript, and as well creating a 6 act, separately monologued play.

Contact: bruce.kauffman@hotmail.com

HBP books by Bruce Kauffman

(Order any of these books from e-stores around the world or your local bookstore.)

The Texture of Days, in Ash and Leaf
— ISBN - 978-1-897475-86-7

a seed within
— ISBN - 978-1-897475-99-7

The Silence Before the Whisper Comes
— ISBN - 978-1-897475-89-0

That Not Forgotten - Anthology Editor
— ISBN - 978-1-897475-89-8

"seed" was originally published by:

The Plowman, Whitby, ON
2005

ISBN-1-55072-743-5

Cover Photographer Bio:

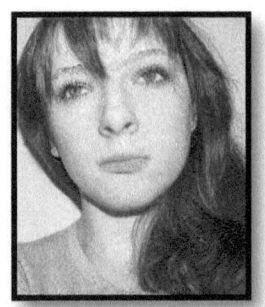

Eleanor Leonne Bennett is a young internationally award winning photographer and artist who has won first place awards with National Geographic, The World Photography Organisation, Nature's Best Photography, Papworth Trust, Mencap, The Woodland Trust and Postal Heritage. Her photography has been published in the Telegraph, The Guardian, the BBC News Website and on the cover of books and magazines in the United states and Canada.

Her artwork is exhibited globally, with her work having been shown in London, Paris, Indonesia, Los Angeles, Florida, Washington, Scotland, Wales, Ireland, Canada, Spain, Germany, Japan, Australia and twice exhibited with The CIWEM Environmental Photographer of the year Exhibition. She has also received coverage on ABC television and national British radio.

www.ingramcontent.com/pod-product-compliance
Lightning Source LLC
Chambersburg PA
CBHW021131080526
44587CB00012B/1229